THE
STANDARD
REUNIFICATION
METHOD

SRM
V3

REUNIFY

A Practical Method to Unite Students with Parents After an Evacuation or Crisis.
The "I Love U Guys" Foundation

PEACE

It does not mean to be in a place where there is no noise, trouble, or hard work.

It means to be in the midst of those things and still be calm in your heart.

STANDARD REUNIFICATION METHOD

SRM V3 CHANGE HISTORY

AUTHOR/CONTRIBUTOR	VERSION	REVISION DATE	REVISION COMMENTARY
John-Michael Keyes	0.9.0	2011-09-17	Preliminary Draft
John-Michael Keyes	0.9.1	2011-10-01	First Final Contest Revision
Ellen Stoddard-Keyes	0.9.2	2011-10-16	Preliminary Edits
Lee Shaughnessy	0.9.3	2011-10-26	Preliminary Edits
Joseph Majsak	1.0	2011-11-16	Continuity and Final Edits
John-Michael Keyes	1.1	2016-06-08	Additional Content
John-Michael Keyes Will Schwall Michelle Brady Russ Deffner Carolyn Mears	2.0	2017-03-02	Reunifier replaces Runner Additional Content Edits
Kevin Burd Ellen Stoddard-Keyes Allyson Jones Melissa A. Reeves, Ph.D, NCSP, LCMHC	3.0	2023-03-27	Updates and Edits Update ICS / HSEEP Compatibility Update Communication Recommendations NASP Guidance

The Standard Reunification Method
A Practical Method to Unite Students with Parents After an Evacuation or Crisis
The "I Love U Guys" Foundation
Version 3.0
ISBN - 978-1-951260-12-5

DEDICATION

The "I Love U Guys" Foundation dedicates this book to the many people who have invested time, knowledge and caring toward the art of safely and responsibly re-uniting students, guardians and families when daily routines are disrupted.

FORWARD

The concept for the Standard Reunification Method (SRM) isn't new. There are many resources available to design a well-run reunification, however few have all the parts in one place. The SRM is a synthesis of common practices in use at a number of districts, departments, and agencies, as well as guidance provided by a variety of federal governmental agencies.

The evolution of SRM has included reviews, comments, and suggestions from a number of practitioners. As of 2023, the SRM has been subjected to tactical scrutiny by hundreds of law enforcement agencies and operational review and adoption by thousands of schools.

ACKNOWLEDGMENTS

The "I Love U Guys" Foundation is primarily grateful to Will Schwall, Emergency Manager, Hays County Sheriff's Office, San Marcos, Texas, for the structure and organization of the materials, and Michelle Brady, Emergency Planning Coordinator, Hillsboro School District, Hillsboro, Oregon, for inspiring the job action sheets.

STAFF

At the time of this version release, The "I Love U Guys" employs eight people full time, all of whom bring unique skills, curiosity and intelligence to these materials.

Allyson Jones, Communications Manager, Andy Arnold, Instructor/Explorer, Brooke Weeber, Directors' Assistant, Carly Posey, Mission Director, Emily Pisqui, Administrative Assistant, Ellen Stoddard-Keyes, Operations Director, and John-Michael Keyes, Executive Director.

BOARD OF DIRECTORS

Whereas many nonprofits have a combative relationship with their Boards, we have always treasured ours for their input, dedication and wisdom.

Chris Zimmerman, Craig Straw, Dave Bauer, Frank DeAngelis, Heilit Biehl, James Englert, Louis S. Gonzalez, Murphy Robinson, and Pat Hamilton.

INPUT AND GUIDANCE

We are grateful to the following people who helped with additional, indirect guidance for the Standard Reunification Method:

Pat Hamilton – Chief Operating Officer, Adams 12 Five Star Schools, Adams County, CO

Bill Godfrey - C3 Pathways
https://www.c3pathways.com

Kevin Burd, Priority of Life Training and Consulting
https://priorityoflife.org

ADJUNCT INSTRUCTORS

The Foundation has a growing pool of skilled and trained instructors who conduct trainings around the country on a part time basis, bringing their expertise and knowledge to the table. They bring back information, and we work together to stay current and improve the programs.

CONTACT INFORMATION

The "I Love U Guys" Foundation can be reached online at https://iloveuguys.org.

Email: srp@iloveuguys.org

The "I Love U Guys" Foundation
P.O. Box 489, Placitas, NM 87043

REQUEST FOR COMMENT

The Standard Reunification Method is a synthesis of common practices in use at a number of districts, departments, and agencies, as well as guidance provided by a variety of federal governmental agencies.

The evolution of SRM has included reviews, comments, and suggestions from a number of practitioners. As of 2023, the SRM has been subjected to tactical scrutiny by hundreds of law enforcement agencies and operational review and adoption by thousands of schools.

Suggestions for modification can be made via email at srm_rfc@iloveuguys.org. Please include contact information, district, department, or agency, including daytime phone.

"Recovery starts before the crisis begins."

"Reunification is the first step in the recovery process."
– John McDonald, Executive Director of Safety and Emergency Planning,
Jeffco R1, Colorado

TABLE OF CONTENTS

MISSION

The "I Love U Guys" Foundation was created to restore and protect the joy of youth through educational programs and positive actions in collaboration with families, schools, communities, organizations, and government entities.

THE "I LOVE U GUYS" FOUNDATION

On September 27th, 2006 a gunman entered Platte Canyon High School in Bailey, Colorado, held seven girls hostage, and ultimately shot and killed Emily Keyes. During the time she was held hostage, Emily sent her parents text messages... "I love you guys" and "I love u guys. k?"

Emily's kindness, spirit, fierce joy, and the dignity and grace that followed this tragic event define the core of The "I Love U Guys" Foundation.

COMMITMENT

There are several things we are committed to. The most important thing we can do is offer our materials at no cost to schools, districts, departments, agencies, and organizations. The reason we are able to continue to provide this service is due, in part, to the generosity of our donors and Mission Partners (see Partner with Love www.iloveuguys.org). The "I Love U Guys" Foundation works very hard to keep our costs down as well as any costs associated with our printed materials. Donor and Mission Partner support allows us to stretch those dollars and services even more. Your gift, no matter the size, helps us achieve our mission. Your help makes a difference to the students, teachers, first responders, and the communities in which we live and work.

WARNINGS AND DISCLAIMER

Every effort has been made to make this book as complete and accurate as possible, but no warranty or fitness is implied. The information provided is on an "as is" basis. Please visit our website (https://iloveuguys.org) for detailed information.

COPYRIGHTS AND TRADEMARKS

In order to protect the integrity and consistency of The Standard Reunification Method, The "I Love U Guys" Foundation exercises all protection under copyright and trademark. Use of this material is governed by the Terms of Use or a Commercial Licensing Agreement.

COMMERCIAL LICENSING

Incorporating the SRM into a commercial product, like software or publication, requires a commercial license. Please contact The "I Love U Guys" Foundation for more information and costs.

ABOUT THIS BOOK

In 2012, The "I Love U Guys" Foundation introduced the Standard Reunification Method. At the time, we saw a void in school safety planning regarding student/parent reunification after an incident. We were certain this was a true need, but few schools or districts actually had reunification plans and practices in place. Fewer still had actually drilled or practiced.

Was it truly a need? The answer lies in the widespread adoption of the SRM. Since 2012, thousands of schools in the US and Canada have implemented the Standard Reunification Method as a means to safely reunite students and families after a crisis.

Recovery starts before the crisis begins. Reunification is one step in that recovery.

This is Version 3.0 of the Standard Reunification Method. But notice, we use the word method. Not protocol. Not procedure. Method.

What that means is that we provide you with some tactics. Things we know. But the incident, your reunification site, and your environment, will ultimately dictate what you do.

Please, in your planning, if you see something here that doesn't seem to work in your environment, figure out what does. Let us know.

ABOUT SRM V3

Version 3 contains expanded guidance, closer adherence to FEMA Incident Command System, and compatibility with HSEEP (Homeland Security Exercise and Evaluation Program) 2020.

Although SRM Version 2 is still valid, The I Love U Guys Foundation recommends updating to the newer version when possible.

THE "I LOVE U GUYS" FOUNDATION MOU

Some schools, districts, departments, and agencies may also desire a formalized Memorandum of Understanding (MOU) with The "I Love U Guys" Foundation. For a current version of the MOU, please visit https://iloveuguys.org.

The purpose of this MOU is to define the responsibilities of each party and provide scope, and clarity of expectations. It affirms the agreement of stated protocol by schools, districts, departments, and agencies. It also confirms the online availability of the Foundation's materials.

An additional benefit for the Foundation is in seeking funding. Some private grantors view the MOU as a demonstration of program effectiveness.

TERMS OF USE

Schools, districts, departments, agencies, and organizations may use these materials, at no cost, under the following conditions:

1. Materials are not re-sold.
2. Notification of use is provided to The "I Love U Guys" Foundation through one of the following:
    2.1 Email notice of use to srm@ilove.uguys.org
    2.2 Memorandum of Understanding
3. The following modification to the parent handouts and reunification cards are allowable:
    3.1 Localization

FAIR USE POLICY

These materials are for educational and informational purposes only and may contain copyrighted material the use of which has not always been specifically authorized by the copyright owner. In accord with our nonprofit mission, we are making such material available for the public good to restore and protect the joy of youth through educational programs and positive actions in collaboration with families, schools, communities, organizations, and government entities.

The "I Love U Guys" Foundation IRS 501(c)3 est. 2006 asserts this constitutes a 'fair use' of any such copyrighted material as provided in Section 107 of the US Copyright Law. In accordance with Title 17 U.S.C. Section 107, these materials are distributed without profit to those who have expressed a prior interest in receiving the included information for criticism, comment, news reporting, teaching, scholarship, education, and research.

If you wish to use copyrighted material from this site for purposes of your own that go beyond fair use, you must obtain permission from the copyright owner.

If your copyrighted material appears in our materials and you disagree with our assessment that it constitutes 'fair use,' contact us.

PRIVACY POLICY

When you agree to the Terms of Use by sending an MOU, your contact information will be entered into a database. You will receive notifications when there are updates and/or new materials. You will have the opportunity to opt in to receive periodic blog posts and newsletters via email.

Our Commitment to Program Users: We will not sell, share or trade names, contact, or personal information with any other entity, nor send mailings to our donors on behalf of other organizations. This policy applies to all information received by The "I Love U Guys" Foundation, both online and offline, as well as any electronic, written, or oral communications. Please see our website for the full Privacy text.

"Cops own the crime. Fire owns the flames. Schools own the kids."

"But Paramedics own the patient."

And that may be an area of conflict during an incident.

Your reunification plans and methods must be communicated with first responders prior to an incident.

REUNIFICATION

The nation has experienced high-profile acts of school violence. In response to this and the everyday types of crises, The "I Love U Guys" Foundation develops programs to help districts, departments and agencies respond.

One critical aspect of crisis response is accountable reunification of students with their parents or guardians in the event a controlled release is necessary. The Standard Reunification Method provides school and district safety teams with proven methods for planning, practicing, and achieving a successful reunification. Keep in mind though, that this is an evolving process. While there is a smattering of science in these methods, there is certainly more art. Site-specific considerations will dictate how these practices can be integrated into school and district safety plans. Successful planning and implementation will also demand partnerships with all responding agencies participating in a crisis response.

ADAMS 12, FIVE STAR SCHOOLS METHOD

The methods detailed in the first version of the Standard Reunification Method are based on the practices developed at the Adams 12, Five Star School District, Thornton, Colorado, by Pat Hamilton, Chief Operating Officer, and also at Jefferson County School District, Golden, Colorado, by John McDonald, Executive Director of Security and Emergency Planning.

Since its introduction in 2012, other districts and agencies have also contributed.

The core concept of the Adams 12 Reunification Method rests on accountability achieved through a process based on managing the physical location of students, staff, and incoming parents. The process also uses perforated cards. These cards are completed by parents or guardians at the reunification site. The cards are separated at the perforation, and a reunifier retrieves the child.

OBJECTIVES

The objective of this manual is to help districts develop, train, and mobilize a district reunification team, and implement tangible, on-site, and off-site reunification plans. Inherent in this objective is creating or strengthening partnerships with responding agencies – police, fire, and medical. By having school and district personnel build a well-designed draft plan, it becomes easier to engage the responders and other key participants in the planning process. During this process, a core philosophy is essential:

Cops own the crime.
Fire owns the flames.
Schools own the kids.
Paramedics own the patient.

Additionally, performing a successful reunification is much more likely when drills are conducted in advance of an event. Tabletop exercises and live exercises should be scheduled and performed.

WHAT DOES IT COST?

Implementing the Standard Reunification Method concepts and planning stages take a certain amount of time. But in the grand scheme of school safety, the level of effort is modest. There will be some staff hours committed to the planning, training, and practice of these concepts. There will be some cost in printing, and in creating both the ROK boxes (Reunification Operation Kits) and the classroom "go kits" necessary for successful reunification.

"Go kits" are the bags or folders that teachers need in their classrooms during any type of event. They often include class rosters, tissues, space blankets, candy for low blood sugar, and other items specific to the location and students. ROK Boxes are typically maintained at the district level and contain everything necessary for the reunification team to function.

Visit https://iloveuguys.org/ to find links for all materials found in the ROK box. Since some of this activity is happening at the district level, the cost of the kits can be spread among all of the schools in the district.

WHEN TO INITIATE A REUNIFICATION

Initiating a reunification can be a result of anything abnormal at the school that renders it unsafe to stay in, or something in the area such as a power or phone outage, weather event, hazmat incident, bomb threats, criminal activity in the area, or active violence at the school.

In some cases, it may be only a partial student population reunification. For instance, criminal activity in the area might result in reunifying students who walk to and from school. In other instances, reunification of the entire student population may be necessary for things such as a gas leak in the school or a violent event.

WHY BOTHER?

Crisis recovery starts before the crisis, not after. Simply "winging it" when reuniting ignores not only the mental health demands that accompany a crisis, but the responsibility of the school and the district to maintain the chain of custody for every student.

No school is immune to stuff hitting the proverbial fan. Wild land or structural fires, hazardous materials, floods, tornados, blizzards, power outages, tsunamis, bomb threats, acts of violence, acts of terror... these just start the list of events that may necessitate a controlled reunification and release for a school or district.

A predetermined, practiced reunification method ensures the reunification process will not further complicate what may already be a chaotic, anxiety-filled scene. In fact, putting an orderly reunification plan into action will help prevent emotions from escalating at the site.

There is a hidden side effect of implementing the Standard Reunification Method. Going through the planning and training process may help strengthen district relationships with first responders. Often law enforcement is active in partnering with schools and districts. Less often is the fire department. The SRM may be a vector for strengthening relationships with fire agencies as well.

THE PROCESS IN A NUTSHELL

The materials in this manual provide the fundamentals for a comprehensive district plan. The beauty of the Standard Reunification Method is its simplicity.

- Establish a parent/guardian check-in location.
- Deliver the students to an assembly area or a transportation area beyond the field of vision of parents/guardians.
- Conduct accountability, or attendance, of who is at the assembly area (student and staff).
- Once students are on-site, notify parents/guardians of the location.
- "Greeters" hand parents/guardians a Reunification Card, and help them understand the process.
- The parent/guardian completes the card and brings it to the check-in area. The procedure allows parents/guardians to self-sort during check-in, streamlining the process.
- Parent/guardian identification is verified. The card is split at the perforation, and the parent/guardian receives the bottom portion.
- Parent/guardian brings that to an area outside the student assembly area and hands it to a "Reunifier."
- The "Reunifier" recovers a student from the assembly area and delivers them to the parent/guardian.
- Controlled lines of sight allow for an orderly flow, and issues can be handled with less drama and anxiety.
- Medical, notification or investigative contingencies are anticipated.
- Pedestrian "flows" are created so lines don't cross.
- In the end, successful reunification is about managing the student and parent experience.

COMMON QUESTIONS

Who is allowed to pick up students?

This comes down to a local school or district policy. Some schools allow anyone on the emergency contact form to pick up the child. Others limit it to only primary guardians if the reunification is due to a violent event. Your organization will have to think through the process and develop a local policy.

What about kids with multiple guardians, homes, or from multiple families?

It will be essential for schools to communicate with all guardians who may pick up a child. This becomes complicated when kids live in different homes depending on the day. You will also run into a situation where one guardian arrives before the other, picks up the child, and never communicates with the other guardians. The school will have to notify the later arriving guardians once they get to the check-in area that the child has already been picked up.

WHY USE CARDS?

Many schools use electronic rosters or campus information systems. Wouldn't that be easier? The reality is a little different. First and foremost is access to data. Foundation research indicates that in any high profile incident, and even many local ones, internet, and cell service become intermittent or even unresponsive. Often school WiFi is impacted as well.

THE CARD

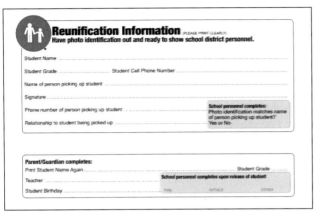

The Reunification Card does a ton of work. Its primary function is to provide accountability, so one student per card is recommended. It also helps with the parent experience. It gives the parent/guardian something to do while they are waiting in line. The card is perforated and gives parents a sense of progress as they go through the process. The main objective is to keep parents/guardians calm and organized while they wait. Let the card do this work for you.

A LITTLE SOCIAL ENGINEERING

A reunification typically occurs because of a crisis or emergency. Consequently, not just students and parents /guardian are trying to function at elevated stress levels; staff, their families, and other first responders also feel the strain.

By having a defined process with signage, cards, branding, procedures, and protocols, the school presents an organized, calm face to all involved. Fear or uncertainty often results from the unknown. By adopting, communicating, and practicing a "known" procedure, the school removes some of that uncertainty.

The cards also bring anxiety down a notch. Asking a parent/guardian to complete the form is a familiar activity and will demand they slow down and perform a cognitive action, "Here, read the instructions on the back, and we'll get things started," might be the first step in lowering blood pressure.

ACCOUNTABILITY: THE ONE NON-NEGOTIABLE

The entire process of reunification, much like any other crisis response method that is based on the National Incident Management System (NIMS) and uses the Incident Command System (ICS), can and should be modified to fit the needs of your local organization. Names and titles can be changed based on what works for you. Ensure all responding agencies understand and are aware of the terminology.

The one thing that cannot be modified is the need for 100% accountability of your students and staff. You absolutely must know who is at the reunification site and who is not. Understand that you may not know the exact location of everyone. This is especially true in a violent event where many will self-evacuate. However, by identifying who is at the impacted site, who evacuated via transportation, and who arrived at the reunification site, you will be able to determine who is present at the reunification site and who is missing.

The accountability process could look like this: During the evacuation phase of an incident, teachers take attendance of their students. This attendance is collected to include staff members, and gives you the number of staff and students you have at the impacted site. If you started the day with 300 total students and staff and you account for 278 during an evacuation, you now know that you need to locate 22 individuals. You should also be able to identify who those missing individuals are. Remember, just because they are not present does not mean they are injured or deceased, as many people will self-evacuate. You will now know that you must maintain the accountability of 278 individuals as they are transported from the impacted site to the reunification site. This information must be communicated to the incident commander at the reunification site and passed along to the student assembly supervisor. Once the students and staff begin to arrive at the reunification site, they will be accounted for by their student assembly supervisor or an accountant assigned to them. If it was not already done, a name-by-name roster should be developed at this point. You absolutely must know the name of each person who has arrived at the reunification site. Once all 278 individuals arrive, you now know that no more transportation is coming from the impacted site. Be sure to confirm this with the impacted site transport team. The name-by-name roster can then be duplicated, one copy stays with the assembly area supervisor, and a second copy goes to the accountant at the parent check-in area. By using this process, you will now know if a student is at the reunification site when their parent or guardian checks in.

NOT SO WEIRD ADVICE

At first blush, this bit of advice may sound weird to educators: "Check out FEMA. Go to http://training.fema.gov and complete the online training for IS-100.C Introduction to Incident Command System." The course takes about an hour and a half to complete and introduces some basic emergency response principles.

Here's why this advice isn't as weird as it sounds. Every responding agency that partners with schools uses "Incident Command" during a crisis. The Incident Command System (ICS) is a response method that determines the role of everyone responding to a crisis and defines a shared vocabulary and shared expectations of behavior.

District and school safety teams need this shared vocabulary when interacting with first responders during a crisis. Equally important is that, when meeting with first responders, having the concepts and vocabulary of ICS removes some of the language barriers. It also shows a commitment to success that departments and agencies will appreciate.

Finally, understanding ICS concepts allows school or district leadership to become a part of the response structure rather than victims or unused assets. It opens the door to a true unified command where school or district leaders can operate shoulder to shoulder with fire, police, EMS, and other public safety leaders.

INCIDENT COMMAND SYSTEM

Whether it is a man-made or natural crisis, or an act of violence in the school, law enforcement, fire, and medical teams will be involved in the reunification process. Learning to understand and speak a common language as well as being familiar with their procedures is imperative to a successful outcome. With that in mind, district and school safety teams must understand and use the Incident Command System.

The Incident Command System can also be used for pre-planned, non-emergency occasions such as sporting events or large gatherings. All the tasks that need to be completed before and during the event can be put into the ICS structure. The structure provides a way to better organize tasks and personnel.

PRIORITIES, OBJECTIVES, STRATEGIES, AND TACTICS

A valuable FEMA resource is the Incident Action Planning Guide, and it's a good start in understanding how first responders manage an incident.

From a school or district perspective, it's important to understand that the Incident Commander has an expectation that to be useful during the event, the school or district personnel need to have some experience with incident command.

If the school or district personnel don't exhibit any knowledge of the process, their input may be marginalized.

ARTICULATE YOUR P.O.S.T.

The first step in incident management is defining the priorities, objectives, strategies, and tactics that will be used during the incident. While each one will be unique, there are considerations that can be addressed in advance.

Priorities:
- Student and staff safety and well-being.
- Student and staff whereabouts and condition.
- Starting the recovery process.

Objectives:
- Every student has been accounted for.
- Every staff member has been accounted for.
- Every student still in the school's control is reunited with their parent or guardian.

Strategies:
- The Standard Reunification Method

Tactics:
- Tactics will vary based on the event and the environment but look at the typical reunification lifecycles on page 16 for a jumpstart.

The next pages describe the structure of the Incident Command System and how it functions in schools and districts.

Following that, there are examples of what the roles might look like during different types of reunifications. Please refer to the Resources and References page at the back of this book for clarification of some of the terms used.

INCIDENT COMMMAND ROLES

These are the different roles people will take during a reunification. On the following pages, various types of reunifications are described. There are explanations of unique considerations for each type of reunification, and how the groups can be activated and used.

Incident Commander

A school Principal is very likely to be the initial Incident Commander. When something unexpected happens (call it an incident) which changes the daily routine, they assess the situation and determine what actions need to be taken. When it will require a responsible reunification of students with parents or guardians, a number of steps are taken.

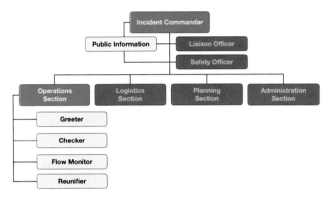

The Incident Commander coordinates Priorities, Objectives, Strategies, and Tactics for an accountable and organized reunification of students with parents/guardians. They decide which key staff stakeholders will be needed, and ensure that notification has been made to them for activation. They will establish security measures for everyone in the school.

However, they do not do it alone. While the Incident Commander is the central point of contact they are eventually surrounded by a team of support. As people arrive to assist, they assign them to manage specific areas as necessary based on the type of incident. They will assign command staff, who fill very specific roles, as well as section chiefs. The typical sections of the incident command system are Operations, Planning, Logistics, and Administration.

Command Staff

The command staff assists the incident commander with communications, safety oversight (to make sure you do not end up with another incident within your incident), and a liaison to ensure integration with other organizations.

Section Chiefs

Section Chiefs, often referred to as the General Staff, report directly to the Incident Commander. They subdivide the incident and assign additional personnel as needed to achieve their objectives. Some, such as Finance/Administration, won't need to be staffed at all during a school-based incident.

Example: In an on-site reunification for a non-violent incident, the Incident Commander assigns an **Operations Section Chief** who oversees the people conducting the reunification. The reunification team provides Section Chiefs with status and resource information, who in turn report to the Incident Commander. The number of subordinates a school needs will depend on how many students they need to reunite. In a large reunification, the Operations Chief may assign Leads for each group, and the Leads will report to the Chief.

This example assumes that the students are in the main assembly area with their classes, and supervised by their teacher. The decision to engage Logistics or Planning is made by the Incident Commander. If they see a need to acquire or provide supplies such as water or snacks, they might assign someone to Logistics to handle that. In non-violent events, these roles can usually be filled by school staff or may not be needed.

Span of Control

The term "span of control" refers to how many people a single individual can supervise. The recommended span of control is one person supervising no more than seven people, with two to five being the ideal number.

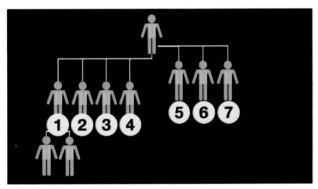

People in various roles will report to the person who is assigned as their commander/supervisor. This keeps communication clear and allows for accurate responses.

It is important to note that the ICS structure is not set in stone. It is adaptable and jobs, names, and section responsibilities can be adjusted to fit the needs of your organization and location. It is imperative, however, that if changes are made to the traditional model they are articulated to other local authorities and you practice regularly with them to ensure everyone is on the same page.

COMMUNICATION

In any type of event, clear and well-planned communication is essential to providing the right information while mitigating the stress of the situation. Depending on the type of incident, you might have only minutes to prepare a statement and communicate it to the appropriate people.

Communication with parents and guardians is critical to the reunification process. Once students and staff are at the reunification site and you are ready to begin the reunification process, a multi-channel message is sent to parents and/or guardians regarding where reunification will take place and what they need to bring with them.

PUBLIC INFORMATION OFFICER (PIO)

The role of **Public Information Officer** is filled by a staff member who usually handles outward communication. No matter how small the incident, the fact that a school day has been disrupted means they are obligated to keep parents and the public informed of the status of the situation.

It is critical for the school and district to ask parents and guardians to update their contact information routinely.

Parents and/or guardians are contacted using the communication method that's best for their school community. Use a push method (text, email, phone) and a passive method such as posting on social media.

Throughout the year, routinely ask parents to update their contact information, and ask them to appoint a trusted friend or neighbor as a backup contact. That is especially important when parents might have a job that restricts their ability to leave, be available by phone, or requires a long commute.

Joint Information Center

The physical location of the JIC will be determined by the Incident Commander in consultation with the Lead PIO. It is common to locate the JIC away from the crisis site to ensure access to reliable utilities (power, phone, Internet, etc.) and help minimize press congregating at the crisis site.

This can be busy and focused. It will include a few resources who will be working together to deliver clear and consistent messaging as approved by the Incident Commander.

Unless a backup plan for internet service is in place at the crisis site, internet will fail quickly. This affects security cameras and phones if they are VoIP (Voice over Internet Protocol) based.

CHANNELS

Decide which methods of communication are the best fit for your community. This depends on your community's internet bandwidth, cell phone service, and other preferences. Whatever you choose needs to be reliable, fast, and reach a high percentage of community members quickly. Document who on the Communication Team has access to update each channel.

Also, think about which channels are used regularly for day-to-day messaging, like emails. When sending out messages regarding reunification, consider using alternative methods such as text and phone, which may not be used as frequently. Doing so will alert the recipients that this is not the regular, daily email but something more important.

SCHOOL-BASED MENTAL HEALTH PROFESSIONALS

Many schools have mental health professionals as part of their team, and they can be an incredible asset during any type of reunification. An evacuation and reunification can cause stress or anxiety regardless of the reason it was conducted. Therefore, it is important that mental health professionals are on-site and ready to assist.

During a larger reunification, and especially for those occurring due to a violent event, a district-level mental health supervisor should be put in place to oversee mental health services at the reunification site. This Supervisor should work with the incident command staff to ensure mental health services are available for students and staff. Oftentimes those can be placed in or near the student assembly area. Additionally, mental health professionals need to be made available for parents/guardians who are waiting in line. Finally, they should also be at the check-in area to assist families who are notified their student is not at the reunification site.

PREPARATION

A tabletop exercise is a great start; basically, it's a brainstorming session. Your Communication Team talks through possible scenarios and formulates messaging accordingly. They must think about what immediate information is necessary, how to follow up, and who they will need to speak with/follow to receive trusted updates.

Use the 27/9/3 rule during message preparation. This is a very basic recommendation and suggests using a total of 27 words, which can be spoken in about nine seconds, containing three or fewer key points.

The team should pre-script some basic messages that may be sent out, with blank spaces for details like time and date. Having these pre-approved and available will aid the team later if they're under stress or time constraints.

THE DISTRICT REUNIFICATION TEAM

Reunification will take place for a variety of reasons. It's a good bet that at some point today a school somewhere is having to conduct a reunification of students with their appropriate caregivers. Most often, reunification will be needed for non-traumatic, non-violent events, such as a power outage, heating loss, or a weather-related event. In these cases, the school typically handles the reunification duties on their own with little to no outside support. However, during larger, more complex incidents district support will be needed to assist the schools.

Offsite reunification on the other hand will most likely require District resources and it is a good practice to have a central Reunification Team staffed by District personnel. There are several reasons for this:

- Training can be more readily coordinated.
- Experienced teams are more proficient.
- School-based teams may initially be unavailable.

Smaller districts may recruit from various school administrators to populate the team. Extremely small districts may recruit volunteers from the community to staff the Reunification Team. A good rule of thumb for team size is five people, plus one per 100 students.

Once the staff is at the reunification site, there are roles they will assume for setup, breakdown, and the actual reunification.

REUNIFICATION ROLES AND DUTIES

The following outlines the roles and duties of the Reunification Team. Not all these roles need to be filled for every reunification. For detailed tasks see the Job Action Sheets found at https://iloveuguys.org/The-Standard-Reunification-Method.html

Accountant Assemble rosters of who is on site and assist in identifying missing students or staff. In a very small reunification, one person can fill the role of Accountant and Checker.

Checkers Verify ID and that the person is on the emergency contact roster. Direct parents to the accountant or the Reunification Area.

Check-in Area Supervisor Establishes and manages the check-in process. Supervises checkers and accountants.

Class Leaders Teachers and Staff who arrive with students remain in the Student Assembly Area to manage students. Additional people may be assigned to this task.

Communications Facilitate radio and other communication needs. May be combined with the PIO.

Exit Accountant Collects bottom slip of reunification card and checks students out once reunified. Can be combined with Exit Director role.

Exit Director The final person the students and parent/guardian see during the reunification process. They are available to answer any questions. Their most important role is to be a friendly face who offers a wave or hug. Often the school principal likes to fill this role. Can be combined with exit accountant.

Facilities Coordinate any physical plant needs.

Finance/Administration Chief Establish and manage administrative staff.

Flow Monitor Assist with guiding traffic flow and assisting parents/guardians as needed.

Greeters Help coordinates the parent lines. Tell parents about the process. Help verify parents without ID. Your most friendly staff members are good in this role.

Greeter Supervisor Establishes and manages the greeting area, Supervises greeters.

Liaison Officer Communicate with Fire, Medical or Law Enforcement.

Logistics Chief Establish and manage logistical staff.

Medical Staff Nurses or EMS personnel on-site

Mental Health Supervisor Oversees the coordination of mental health practitioners from a variety of agencies.

Nutrition Services Provide snacks and water.

Operations Chief Establish and manage operational staff.

Planning Chief Establish and manage planning staff.

Public Information Officer Communicate with parents and press, if appropriate. Coordinate use of mass calls or text messages. May be combined with the communications role.

Reunification Incident Commander Coordinates Priorities, Objectives, Strategies, and Tactics for an accountable, easy reunification of students with parents.

Reunifier Take the bottom of the Reunification Card to Assembly Area, locate the student and bring them to Reunification Area. Ask the student, "Are you okay going home with this person?" There's a lot of walking involved, so consider that when assigning people to this role.

Reunification Area Supervisor Establishes and manages the reunification area. Supervises reunifies.

Safety Officer Observe site and remedy safety concerns.

Scribe Document events. A yellow pad is sufficient.

Student Assembly Supervisor Establish and manage the Student Assembly Area.

Supervisor For span of control, some groups may need Supervisors.

Transportation Directs transportation needs. May become a supervisor position.

Victim Advocates/Mental Health Professionals Standby unless needed.

ON-SITE PARTIAL REUNIFICATION
Incident Command Structure
This chart is an example of the organizational structure that might be used to conduct an On-site Partial Reunification.

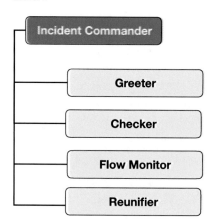

Partial reunification is conducted when only part of the student body will need to be reunited, and very often results from a school being in Secure Protocol. It may be needed at the conclusion of a school day when there is an ongoing hazardous condition outside the school or in the area. It may be due to criminal activity in the area, or a local hazard that makes it unsafe for the students who usually walk home to do so.

Students who ride the bus home would still do so. If there is criminal activity in the area, the bus loading area will require elevated situational awareness and extra staff.

In some rural communities this might only involve a few students, whereas in many urban schools it might be majority of the student population in which case the number of roles as described on page 17 would be expanded.

Schools and districts should conduct a tabletop exercise in advance to talk through the potential hazards and discuss how to manage them.

Student Drivers
The age of the students will play a big role in how the school handles this. High school-age students will be able to manage much more independently than the younger students. Make a plan to address those who drive to and from school, and any students who carpool with them.

Workflow
A partial reunification can typically be successfully completed quickly with the school staff. However, there may be increased law enforcement nearby, and they may be available to assist. The minimum number of recommended roles is five people, plus one per 100 students. to conduct this.

Students may either stay in a room with their teacher or be brought to an assembly area. In the assembly area, students remain with their teacher and classmates to maintain accountability. Discuss this in advance to decide what works best for your school.

We recommend parents and guardians show identification when they arrive at a check-in location. This ensures the correct person is picking up the student. Additionally, it displays an organized, thought-out process that will help maintain order and control in a potentially uncertain situation.

It's not uncommon to have a few students left if all parents cannot be located. It is the schools' and districts' responsibility to plan for this.

Communication
Notification of danger outside the school is usually received by the school from local public safety partners. If this is the case, keep lines of communication open throughout the duration of the incident to monitor events. If the situation is not resolved or minimized by the normal release time, students may be held until it's safe enough to release the buses and for parents to pick up the students who normally walk home.

Contact parents as soon as the problem is identified, let them know the students are safe inside, and the day will proceed as usual except that activities normally held outdoors will be held indoors. Set expectations as clearly as possible to keep stress levels down. This includes telling students what is happening and why you're using the Secure action.

If there is ongoing criminal activity in the area, parents and volunteers are discouraged from coming to the school, as that would put them in harm's way. If the situation becomes more manageable, the school might allow for monitored entry and controlled release. Communicate this to parents. There will be instances when a parent has arranged to pick up their child for an appointment during the day. Depending on what's going on and the information available, the school will have to decide how to handle that.

ON-SITE FULL REUNIFICATION

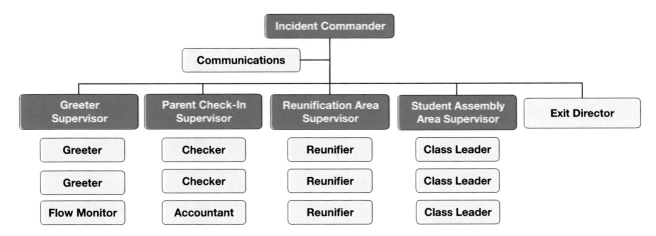

Incident Command Structure

The chart above is an example of the organizational structure that might be used to conduct an On-site Full Reunification. Remember, the minimum recommendation is five people, plus one per 100 students. The additional personnel per 100 students will typically fill more checker, greeter, reunifier, or flow monitor roles as needed. If available, the exit director role can also be filled.

The above chart shows the Incident Commander, a communications individual, and all of the Operations Section roles. In this example, the Incident Commander oversees the Operations Section directly. There is no Planning, Finance, or Logistics section. If these roles became necessary, the Incident Commander could assign them as needed.

An on-site reunification is for an event such as a power outage, water system or mechanical failure, which disrupts school operations. The event is small enough that the school isn't in danger but significant enough that it's not safe to continue operations for the remainder of the school day, and students will leave at an unusual time.

Sending students home on buses may not be a good plan because they could be arriving at locked and empty houses.

As with partial reunification, be sure to develop a plan for students who drive and those who ride with them.

Workflow

A full on-site reunification can often be completed by school staff but they may request assistance from the District. Again, students may either stay in a room with their teacher or be brought to an assembly area. In the assembly area, students remain with their teacher and classmates to maintain accountability. Discuss this in advance to decide what works best for your school.

Utilize the same parent/guardian identification method recommended for partial on-site reunification. Nothing changes in the process between the two types of reunifications, but it does expand with more support staff and more students to reunite.

Communication

Parent/guardian notification for an on-site reunification can most often be handled by the affected school staff. If needed, district personnel should be available to support.

Once it is determined that an unplanned dismissal will be occurring, the school initiates the preplanned communication protocol. Typically this involves phone calls, email, and text messages to parents and guardians. Inform them of the issue and why the change in dismissal time is occurring. It is important to inform them of the reason to avoid any unnecessary confusion or panic.

Even though the incident may not seem like a big event, be prepared for the media to arrive. Often times a story involving a school will fit nicely in the day's news cycle. Ensure staff is properly trained and briefed on what to say. Things like "we were well trained to conduct the reunification and are following our plan" will sound much better than "we were caught off guard but we are figuring it out." Having a well thought out and practiced plan will make everyone more at ease and that mindset will show during any media coverage.

OFF-SITE REUNIFICATION OVERVIEW

During an offsite reunification, as described on the following pages, there will be two separate teams. The district reunification team will deploy to the reunification site while a second team will go to the impacted school. This second team will facilitate transportation and initiate accountability processing. They are responsible for the safe evacuation and transportation of students, teachers, and staff to the reunification site whether it's a walking or driving location.

During a non-traumatic event, school staff may be able to serve as the impacted site team. After a traumatic event, however, they may not be able to fill those roles so it's recommended that the district sets up and trains the two-team method. Law enforcement should also be included in this training as district teams may not be able to get to the scene and it is imperative that accountability and transportation occur in an orderly and normalized process.

> **NASP Online:**
> **Reunification Following School Evacuation**
> Ideally, the reunification site should be within walking distance so that the school is not dependent on other means of transportation as arranging for buses in the immediate aftermath of a crisis or disaster that requires evacuation can be very challenging. However, in some situations it may be best to evacuate students further away from the site, thus coordination must occur with district and/or community transportation personnel to plan for the use of district transportation in emergency situations. Transportation to and from the reunification site must include explicit consideration of students with disabilities and special needs. For some of these students, an individual evacuation plan may be necessary.

TEACHERS: STAY WITH YOUR STUDENTS

Interviews with safety directors directly impacted by crisis reveal a common thread. Often teachers will group together in the immediate aftermath, or assume their job is done when the police arrive on the scene. It's important to emphasize that teachers remain with their students, and aren't done until all of the students have been reunited with their families.

If possible, have teachers fill the roles of class leaders. This will assist with accountability as the teachers can remain with their students throughout the evacuation and reunification process. If the teachers are unable to fill that role, a pool of additional staff such as teaching assistants should be ready to step in. Teachers may be unable for a variety of reasons. They themselves could be parents and need to retrieve their own children. Additionally, the stress of an evacuation and reunification may impact their abilities to fill the role. Sometimes they will only require a short break, while at other times they need some extended attention.

Be sure to include teachers in the process and training. Inform them of counseling resources beforehand and have mental health professionals available as a part of your reunification team.

IMPACTED SCHOOL: TRANSPORT TEAM

The team at the impacted school has these priorities:

- Assemble a master student roster, teacher roster, and guest roster
- Identify and notify the reunification site
- Provide safe transport of students and staff to the reunification site
- Assign District personnel to go to the receiving health facilities if there are injuries, in coordination with Incident Command.

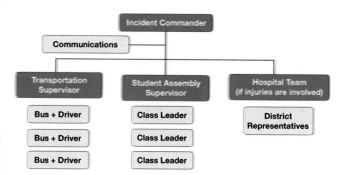

TRANSPORT ROLES AND DUTIES

The following outlines the roles and duties of the Transportation Unit. For detailed tasks see the Job Action Sheets.

Transportation Supervisor: Whether the district runs its own buses or the service is contracted out, the Transportation Supervisor should be involved in all planning, drilling, and training for reunification.

In combination with the Student Assembly Supervisor, coordinate resources (people and vehicles) to execute the safe and accountable movement of students and staff from an impacted site to the reunification site whether it's a walking or driving location.

Supervise an orderly movement of people from the impacted site to the reunification site, and maintain communication with the reunification site about arrivals. Depending on the incident, you may want to keep the bus loading area secure and as uncrowded as possible. After a violent incident, securing the bus loading area will most likely be managed by Law Enforcement personnel.

Class Leaders at the Impacted Site: Report to the Student Assembly Supervisor. Communicate via radio to get students to the transportation area. Most often the Class Leader role is filled by teachers who will remain with the class during evacuation and at the reunification site to maintain accountability and continuity.

Scribe: Document the events. This includes all activities, updates, and actions and the time those took place.

UNIFIED COMMAND OVERVIEW

Unified Command is activated when there are multiple entities with legal authority to be in charge of an incident. For example, law enforcement will have authority in a school violence event, but schools and districts still remain responsible for students and staff (in loco parentis). Unified Command is sometimes used to include key incident stakeholders in decision-making and coordination. The school or district may or may not be viewed as a resource unless prior interaction and training has occurred with public safety partners.

With multiple organizations responding, Leadership of each entity with legal authority communicate with each other and channel information to the Unified Incident Commander.

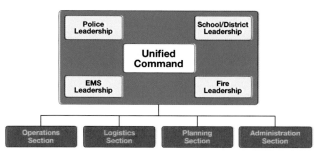

PUBLIC INFORMATION OFFICER (PIO) OR JOINT INFORMATION CENTER (JIC)?

Clear communication, both internal and external, is essential when daily routines are disrupted. Minimally, in non-violent events, external communication is handled by the school or district personnel who usually manage public messaging and social media. This person is your PIO. If the media has a presence, your PIO should be communicating with them to make sure the messaging is agreed upon and consistent.

In larger incidents, and especially when there has been violence, Unified Command is activated, and there will be a Joint Information Center. It will include Law Enforcement and/or Fire PIOs, and often an Investigator alongside the school/district PIO.

The JIC is managed by the Lead Public Information Officer (PIO). As information is obtained, the PIO brings it to Incident Command, and messaging is formulated and delivered.

INCLUDING FIRST RESPONDERS

It is absolutely imperative that as the reunification plan is developed, first responders are brought into the process. Meeting with command staff, including PIOs, both law enforcement and Fire/EMS will generate two outcomes. First, they will look at your plan from their perspective. Second, they have suggestions you might not have thought of.

In the example chart above, police, fire, EMS, and school leadership will sit together and make decisions as a single unit. The decisions will be sent out to the subordinate sections to ensure unified objectives.

LAW ENFORCEMENT SUPPORT

Depending on the type of event, the school may receive an influx of law enforcement officers. During a violent incident, the response might be overwhelming at the impacted site. Ensure that in training prior to an incident, the school, district, and law enforcement leadership is aware of additional need for law enforcement support at the reunification site.

At the reunification site, law enforcement support may be necessary. Some assignments may include:

- Traffic Control
- Crowd Control
- ID Verification
- Perimeter Control
- Security
- Liaison

LOOKING AT REUNIFICATION FROM A LAW ENFORCEMENT PERSPECTIVE

SRM V3 presents a number of organizational structures from a school or district perspective. In the face of an active assailant, when Law Enforcement takes the lead in Unified Command, they may implement an ICS structure supporting the needs of witness interviews, evidence retention and other legal responsibilities.

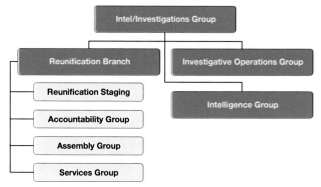

Source: C3Pathways, ASIM - https://c3.cm/asc

WHO ARE VICTIM ADVOCATES?

Many law enforcement agencies, district attorneys, and prosecutors have victim advocates on staff and a cadre of trained volunteers. In many states and counties, they are charged to protect and promote the rights of victims. They often deploy when there is a crisis. Very often they are trained in Psychological First Aid and can be helpful with crisis counseling, if needed, during a reunification. Get to know these community partners.

PARTNERSHIPS

During one Standard Reunification Method workshop conducted by The Foundation, a fire chief requested the training for every fire station in his city. When questioned why, he replied, "We are going to be on the scene. If we're not actively engaged in fire or EMS, we can help with the reunification process." This is a perfect example of a community that is ready to work as a team instead of as separate entities.

OFF-SITE REUNIFICATION - NON-VIOLENT EVENT

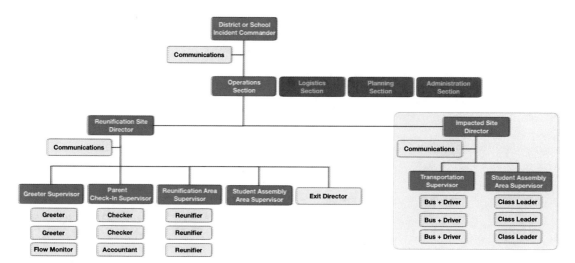

Offsite Non-Violent Event

An off-site reunification is conducted when something happens which makes it unsafe or unhealthy to remain in the building or even a specific area. This could be a gas leak, fire, potential flooding, or something similar.

Transporting students to a different location creates a very different dynamic for parents and families.

The chart above shows an example of the organizational structure that might be used to conduct an evacuation and reunification of the entire student population during a non-violent event.

Workflow

An offsite reunification requires more people simply because there are more moving parts. The minimum recommendation is five people, plus one per 100 students.

While waiting to evacuate, students may either stay in a room with their teacher or be brought to an assembly area. In the assembly area, students remain with their teacher and classmates to maintain accountability. Alternatively, you may choose to move people directly to buses, one classroom at a time.

At the reunification site, we recommend parents and guardians show identification when they arrive to pick up their child. This ensures the correct adult is picking up the student and it displays an organized, thought-out process that will help maintain order and control in a potentially chaotic situation.

It's not uncommon to have a few students left whose parents/guardians cannot make it to the site. It is the schools' and districts' responsibility to have a plan in place fro address that.

Communication

Let parents know as soon as possible, and tell them exactly what is going on and when they might be able to pick up their child. If students will be transported off-site, it's advisable not to immediately tell parents where the site is as parents may cause traffic problems before students and staff arrive.

Preparation

Create relationships in advance with other schools and community partners for reunification sites. It is advisable to create a Memorandum of Understanding with them in order to set expectations and understand responsibilities.

Plan in advance to have a site within walking distance as well as a transport site farther away. The time of day and weather conditions are some of the factors determining which site will be used.

Create classroom go-bags and have them packed with items that your student population requires.

Plan for the accommodations that your students and staff with disabilities may require, making sure to include people with temporary mobility injuries.

Have a plan in place in advance to address high school students who drive to school and/or carpool.

Law Enforcement may be available to assist with safety and traffic control.

Communication Between the Reunification Site and Impacted Site

During a non-violent event requiring evacuation and reunification, the school and district will be responsible for most of the activities. A transport team will be required at the impacted site and a reunification team will be needed at the reunification site.

The District Incident Commander could be located at the reunification site or the impacted school site. It is recommended to go to the reunification site since that location will be operating for the longer period of time.

OFF-SITE REUNIFICATION - VIOLENT EVENT

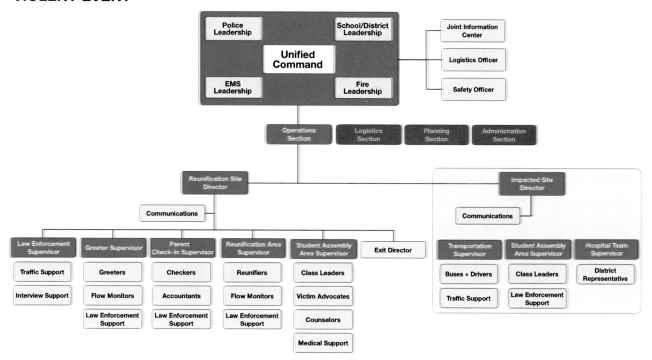

Off-site Violent Event

In the event of violence on campus or in a school, the school must be evacuated because it is now a crime scene. A number of additional resources will arrive, the command structure is adjusted, and extra precautions and actions are necessary.

The chart above shows an example of the organizational structure you may see during a large-scale violent event. What is not shown is the law enforcement, fire, and EMS coordination that will be occurring simultaneously. We only illustrate the reunification specific roles. However, there will be an entire operations section, group, or branch dedicated to tactical response, medical first aid, and evacuation.

This information is here so school safety teams understand this will happen. Acknowledge it and plan for it.

Law Enforcement will arrive and assume command of the impacted site. It is important for both groups to acknowledge that, at this point in time, there are most likely two separate incident command structures which are operating independently. The first is the one initiated by the school in response to the threat or hazard. That structure will be in place prior to the arrival of public safety officials. Once those responders arrive they will initiate their own command structure. As quickly as possible these structures need to be linked up. Eventually, it is likely a Unified Command will be set up. It is crucial that district leadership is a part of the Unified Command.

Workflow

A reunification following a violent event is going to require district support as the impacted school staff may be unavailable. The district reunification team should report to the reunification site and establish communications with incident command.

The school district should be responsible for deciding when it's time to announce the reunification site. Depending on the situation, they may decide to announce it quickly in order to keep parents from arriving at the impacted school.

Evacuation

This discussion assumes that the school is in Lockdown. Law Enforcement most likely will be clearing the classrooms. School personnel should be prepared to assist law enforcement with maps, keys, and information regarding alternative exit pathways to avoid bringing students through, or within sight of, the crime scene(s).

Classrooms can be cleared either to an interior or exterior Assembly Area or directly to a bus if Transportation has been able to get buses there. Either way, every effort should be made to keep the evacuees away from the site of the violence. This could mean bringing some classes to an exit they would not normally use and around the building to the destination.

If body searches are being conducted, if possible find a way for these to occur out of the public's sight.

Move students and staff off-site as quickly as possible while maintaining safety measures. They may arrive at the reunification site before it's set up, in which case they can stay on the buses.

SRP Lifecycle with

EXAMPLE 1: SECURE

Scenario: Criminal activity in the area has resulted in the school going into the Secure protocol. Students were brought into the building. Business as usual inside, but no one is let in or out.

Law enforcement has indicated that school can be released at the normal time even though the situation outside isn't completely resolved.

Considerations: With criminal activity in area of the school, it's decided that students who walk home should have their parents/guardians pick them up.

Incident Command: Because there was no criminal or safety issue in the school, Incident Command would be led by the school safety team. Coordination with Law Enforcement Incident Command about the status of the criminal activity would be necessary.

Public Information Officer: Because the school was not directly involved in criminal activity, the school or district would lead public information within the school community. The District and Law Enforcement PIOs work with the Incident Commander to develop media messaging.

Notifications: Depending on the situation, parents/guardians and media will be notified of what is occurring and the status of student reunification. Additional notification will be made to parents who would need to pick up their students.

Police Role in Reunification: With criminal activity in the area, but not directly near the school, officers may be asked to assist with reunification. Some duties might include assisting with parent/guardian identification (for the parents without ID), traffic control, or simply uniformed presence. Patrol resources may also be relocated near the school.

SECURE LIFECYCLE
- School is placed in Secure Protocol.
- Parents/guardians are notified.
- Business goes on as usual within the school as much as possible.
- Law enforcement presence around the school may be increased.
- At release time, if the situation hasn't been resolved, the Standard Reunification Method is utilized for the students who walk home at the end of school day.

EXAMPLE 2: LOCKDOWN

Scenario: An armed intruder is seen in the school building by a staff member who announces a Lockdown and calls 911. Students and staff immediately take action to avoid injury. The intruder causes damage to the building prior to Law Enforcement arriving.

Considerations: Because it is an active law enforcement response and investigation, the decision is made to transport students to a nearby community center for reunification.

Unified Command: Because it is an active crime scene, law enforcement would establish a unified command with school officials.

Reunification Incident Command: At the reunification site, a command structure is established to manage the reunification.

Joint Information Center: Because it is an active crime scene, the law enforcement PIO would be the primary press representative. The school or district PIO would be in the JIC, communicating with the PIO at the reunification site.

Notifications: Parents/guardians and media are notified that the school has been placed in Lockdown. Additional notifications are made to parents/guardians about the location of the reunification site once students are in route or at the site.

Police Role in Reunification: While the school has become an active crime scene, some officers will be assigned to the reunification site. Depending on the site, police may decide to sweep the area prior to students arriving. In addition to the duties outlined in the Secure example, detectives may be on scene for witness interviews and statements.

LOCKDOWN LIFECYCLE
- School is placed in Lockdown Protocol.
- Multiple law enforcement agencies arrive on scene.
- Parents/guardians begin to arrive outside of the police perimeter.
- Media arrives on scene.
- Internet, WiFi, and cell services become intermittent or unresponsive.
- Police secure the reunification site.
- District mobilizes Reunification Team.
- Buses are deployed and students are transported to the reunification site.
- Parents/guardians are notified of location.
- The Standard Reunification Method is utilized.

Reunification

EXAMPLE 3: EVACUATE

Scenario: An unknown cause has resulted in thick smoke in a school. Students successfully evacuate to the football field.

Considerations: Because it is still an active fire response and investigation, and the area is experiencing inclement weather, a decision is made to transport students to a nearby high school for reunification.

Unified Command: Because it is an active fire event, the fire department would establish unified command with school officials.

Reunification Incident Command: At the reunification site, a command structure is established to manage the reunification.

Joint Information Center: Because it is an active fire event, the fire department PIO would be the primary press representative. The school or district PIO would be in the JIC, communicating with the PIO at the reunification site.

Notifications: Parents/guardians and media are notified that the school has been evacuated. Additional notifications are made to parents/guardians about the location of the reunification site once students are in route or at the site.

Police Role in Reunification: While the school is an active fire scene, the school requests assistance from law enforcement. Officers are assigned to the reunification site.

EVACUATE LIFECYCLE

- Parents/guardians begin to arrive outside the perimeter.
- The media arrive on scene.
- Internet, WiFi, and cell services are intermittent or unresponsive.
- Police secure the reunification site.
- District mobilizes Reunification Team.
- Buses are deployed and students are transported to the reunification site.
- Parents/guardians are notified of site location.
- The Standard Reunification Method is utilized.

EXAMPLE 4: SHELTER

Scenario: A tornado has unexpectedly touched down in a neighborhood. The local elementary school has gone into the Shelter Protocol with all students and staff taking refuge in appropriate locations.

Considerations: The tornado blew down trees and power lines. Roads are closed and there is no access to the school at this time. The school was not damaged but students will need to remain on-site until the roads are cleared and their parents/guardians can arrive.

Unified Command: School officials will be working with the district, local emergency management, law enforcement, public works, and utility companies to clear the roads and get access to the school.

Reunification Incident Command: The school is serving as the reunification site. Since the school was not damaged there was no need for an evacuation. The school staff will serve as the reunification team.

Joint Information Center: The district PIO will work with the town officials to handle communications and notifications.

Notifications: Parents and media are notified that the school was undamaged and all students and staff are safe at this time. Parents will be notified once the roads are cleared and they can pick up their children.

Police Role in Reunification: Law Enforcement will be used to ensure the safety of the tree clearance teams. They may be requested to help with traffic flow in and around the school once the roads are clear.

SHELTER LIFECYCLE

- Shelter Protocol is enacted, students and staff take shelter.
- Shelter is lifted once it is safe
- Notification goes out to parents
- School ensures the safety of the students, and prepares for a reunification
- Routes are cleared
- Parents begin to arrive
- The Standard Reunification Method is utilized.

SRM Staging the

STEP 1
ESTABLISH ONSITE INCIDENT COMMAND

The first step in staging for transport is establishing School Incident Command at the affected school. Integrating with Unified Command should be a priority.

Priorities:	Student and staff safety and wellbeing
	Student and staff whereabouts and condition
	Assemble affected school command staff
	Integrate with Unified Command
	Joint Information Center established
Objectives:	Safe transport of students and staff to reunification site
Strategy:	The Standard Reunification Method
Tactics:	Will be determined by the environment

STEP 2
CLASSROOM EVACUATION

Classrooms are individually evacuated to the Secure Assembly Area. During a Police Led Evacuation, students and staff will be asked to keep their hands visible.

If it is a Police Led Evacuation after a Lockdown, each room will be cleared by Law Enforcement personnel. This process may take up to several hours. Teacher should take attendance in the classroom, prior to evacuation.

SPECIAL NEEDS POPULATIONS

The Individuals with Disabilities Act mandates additional supports for students with special education needs in school setting. These supports would also function to provide supervision and assistance to students with disabilities during emergency situations.

SRM Actions and

COMMUNITY ACTION
PARENTS WILL BEGIN TO ARRIVE

Parents will be arriving at the impacted school. Often with a Lockdown event, adjoining schools will go into Lockout. Parents may be arriving at those schools as well.

REUNIFICATION SITE
MOBILIZE REUNIFICATION TEAM

Contacting the Superintendent and determining the Reunification Site are among the first actions taken. If the site is another school, early release may be necessary.

School for Transport

STEP 3
SECURE ASSEMBLY AREA

At the Secure Assembly Area it is preferable that teachers stay with their students. If some teachers are unable to be at the Secure Assembly Area, doubling up classes with "Partner" teachers is appropriate.

STEP 4
STUDENT AND STAFF TRANSPORT

Students and staff board the bus and are transported to the Reunification Site. Buses having audio video systems can be utilized for further accountability by having students face the camera and state their name.

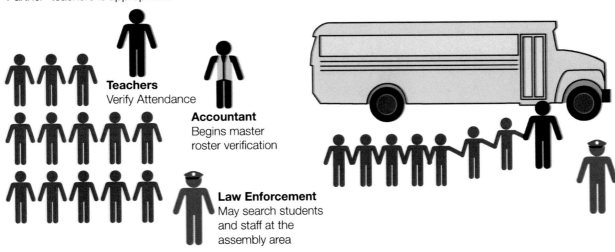

Teachers
Verify Attendance

Accountant
Begins master roster verification

Law Enforcement
May search students and staff at the assembly area

Considerations

LAW ENFORCEMENT
SUPPORT AND INVESTIGATIONS

Regardless of criminal activity, law enforcement support will be necessary at both the impacted school and the reunification site.

FIRE AND EMS
CASUALTY CARE

If necessary, Fire and EMS will establish Casualty Collection, Triage and Transport areas. Many fire departments are also willing to assist in the transport and reunification process, if they are not actively responding to crisis.

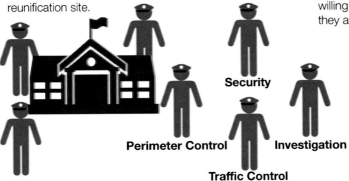

Security

Perimeter Control

Investigation

Traffic Control

SRM Staging the

ASSEMBLY AREA
STUDENTS ENTER OUT OF PARENTAL VIEW

Students are transported to the Reunification Site and are then directed to the Student Assembly Area. Often this is a cafeteria or gymnasium. Upon arrival, students are verified against a master roster.

It is important that students are not in view of their parents when exiting the bus and entering the reunification site.

GREETING AREA
PARENTS ARE MET HERE

As parents arrive, signage directs them to Parent Check-in Table. Greeters begin the process by asking parents to complete the Reunification Card.

Law Enforcement
Often an Officer is posted where students are disembarking.

LE

Student Check-in Table

Law Enforcement Interviews

Student Assembly Area

Transport Students to Site

Helpful Tip
As parents wait for reunification with their student, try to have them clustered rather than in a line. Students may not always be recovered in the order parents line up.

Law Enforcement
Often an Officer is posted where parents wait for reunification.

LE

Parent Reunification Area

Reunification Site

CHECK-IN TABLE
SET UP MULTIPLE LINES
Establish parallel check-in lines based on first initial of last name. Checkers verify ID and custody.

REUNIFICATION AREA
PARENT STUDENT REUNIFICATION
As their tasks are completed, Greeters and Checkers can be reassigned as Reunifiers.

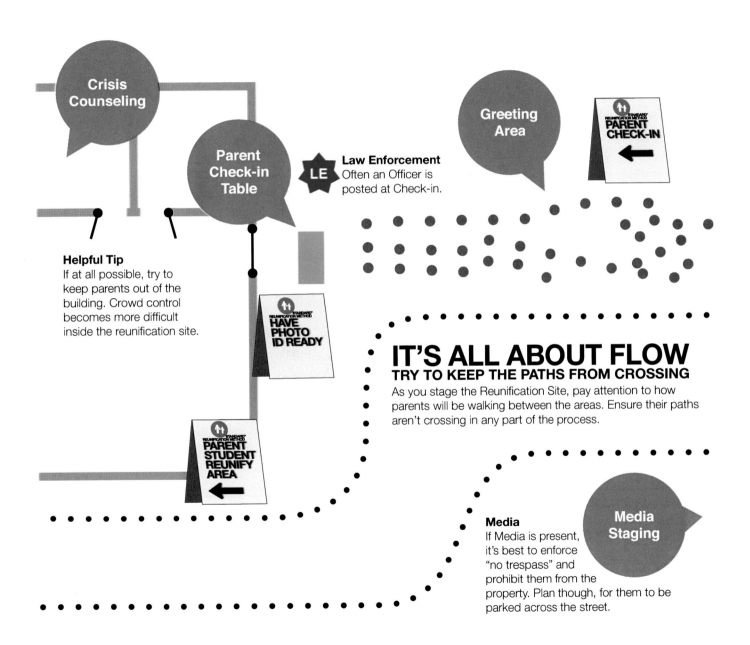

Crisis Counseling

Parent Check-in Table

LE

Law Enforcement
Often an Officer is posted at Check-in.

Greeting Area

PARENT CHECK-IN ←

Helpful Tip
If at all possible, try to keep parents out of the building. Crowd control becomes more difficult inside the reunification site.

HAVE PHOTO ID READY

PARENT STUDENT REUNIFY AREA ←

IT'S ALL ABOUT FLOW
TRY TO KEEP THE PATHS FROM CROSSING
As you stage the Reunification Site, pay attention to how parents will be walking between the areas. Ensure their paths aren't crossing in any part of the process.

Media
If Media is present, it's best to enforce "no trespass" and prohibit them from the property. Plan though, for them to be parked across the street.

Media Staging

SRM The Process

Step 1
Greetings
As parents arrive at the reunification site, Greeters explain the process and distribute Reunification Cards.

Step 2
Parents fill out card
Parents complete the information requested on the card, and begin to self sort into lines.

Step 3
Checkers Verify ID
Parent custody is verified. The card is torn on the perforation and the bottom is returned to the parent. The top is given to the Accountant.

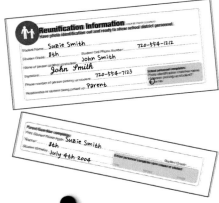

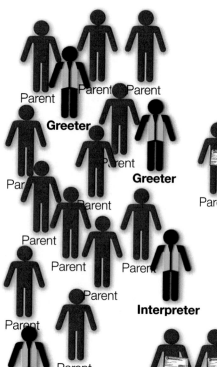

ABC — Checker

DEFGHIJK — Checker

Accountant
The Accountant verifies cards against a master roster and may start sorting cards.

LMN — Checker

Law Enforcement
A uniformed officer can help with crowd control and identity verification.

OPQ..XYZ — Checker

Greeter
Greeters manage the initial intake of parents. They explain the process and answer questions that may arise.

Checker
Checkers verify identification. In some cases custodial authority may need verification as well.

in 6 easy steps

Step 4
Reunification Area
At the Reunification Area, parents give the bottom of the card to a Reunifier. The Reunifier goes to the Assembly area to recover the student.

Step 5
Student Reunification
The Reunifier returns the student to their parents asking the student if they feel comfortable leaving with that adult. They then note the time, and initial the bottom of the card.

Step 6
Accountability
The Reunifier delivers the bottom of the card to the Student Assembly Accountant. The Accountant may start sorting the cards.

Parent   Parent   Parent   **Reunifier**   ● ● ● ●   **Reunifier**   ● ● ● ● Parent   ● ● ● ●   **Reunifier**   **Accountant**

Principal
It may be beneficial to have the school principal in the area where students and parents are reunited.

What If?
the student isn't there?
If the student isn't in the Assembly Area, the Reunifier hands the card to a Victim Advocate/Crisis Counselor.

Separate
the parent from the line
The Victim Advocate/Crisis Counselor then separates the parent from the other parents in line and brings them to a private location.

Law Enforcement
A uniformed officer can help with crowd control and keep the peace.

  Reunifier ● ● ● ● **Counselor** ● ● ● ● **Counselor**      Parent   Parent   Parent   Parent

SRM The Card

REUNIFICATION INFORMATION CARDS

The Standard Reunification Method was created to manage not just the students, but the parental experience of reunification as well. The Reunification Card is an essential element of the method.

Some might initially protest, "What! More Paperwork?" And the answer is "Yes. Precisely." Beyond providing a mechanism for accountability, the card demonstrates to parents that there is a process for this. It shows that school or district has a plan and a method.

The psychology behind the process begins to offer the parent some measure of order in what might be a stressful time. Filling the card out, then separating the top from the bottom, handing the card to the Reunifier, gives the parent feedback, demonstrating progress in the process. The bottom of the card also provides proxy identification for the parent, removing the need to ID them at every phase.

Send it home in advance?

A question often comes up about whether the school should send the cards home in advance and request parents fill out and return them. Certainly an option, but it creates unnecessary work in collecting the cards and diminishes the parent experience. One alternative is to send the cards home, with the handout, and ask parents to complete the card and put it in their car. This gives parents an expectation of the process and some parents will complete the request.

This is available at iloveuguys.org and is also reprinted on page 34.

AVAILABLE IN SPANISH

The Reunification Card is also available in Spanish. Check the website for new translations.

PRESS READY ARTWORK

The Reunification Cards are press ready for your printer. The artwork is set up for Work and Tumble[1] on 8½" x 11" index card stock. Ask your printer for a strong perforation. There is little worse than a "bad perf" on reunification day.

[1] "In prepress and printing, an imposition or layout in which one plate contains all the images (pages) to be printed on both sides of a sheet. When one side of a job has been printed, the pile of printed sheets is turned over, the edge of the sheet that was the gripper edge for the first side becoming the back edge for the second side. After printing, the sheet is cut in half, yielding two identical units."

[1] *Source: PrintWiki – the Free Encyclopedia of Print. http://printwiki.org*

Reunification Information (PLEASE PRINT CLEARLY)
Have photo identification out and ready to show school district personnel.

Student Name ....

Student Grade .... Student Cell Phone Number ....

Name of person picking up student ....

Signature ....

Phone number of person picking up student ....

Relationship to student being picked up ....

School personnel completes:
Photo identification matches name
of person picking up student?
Yes or No

Parent/Guardian completes:

Print Student Name Again.. Student Grade ....

Teacher ....

Student Birthday ....

School personnel completes upon release of student

TIME   INITIALS   OTHER

Parent/Guardian Sign Off
I have read and understand these instructions.

Print Your Name ....

Signature ....

Date ....

Reunification

First, we want to thank you for your patience during this reunification. We share the same goal during this process: Getting you and your student back together as quickly as possible. The reason we're going through this is that an event has occurred at the school that mandates we personally reunite you with your child.

Instructions

1. Please complete the information on the other side of this card.
2. Prepare identification (if you don't have ID with you, please move to the side of the line, it may take a little longer to verify your identity.)
3. Select the check-in line based on either student last name or student grade.
4. After check-in, staff will split this card and a runner will be sent to recover your student. Please step over to the Reunification Location.
5. If there has been injury or other concerns, you may be asked to meet a counselor.
6. Please don't shout at school or district staff. We'll get through this as quickly as possible.

STANDARD REUNIFICATION METHOD

STUDENT/PARENT REUNIFICATION

Circumstances may occur at the school that require parents to pick up their students in a formalized, controlled release. The process of controlled release is called a reunification and may be necessary due to weather, a power outage, hazmat event, danger outside the school or if a crisis occurs at the school. The Standard Reunification Method is a protocol that makes this process more predictable and less chaotic for all involved.

Because a controlled release is not a typical end of school day event, a reunification may occur at a different location than the school a student attends. If this location is another school, then those students may be subject to a controlled release as well.

NOTIFICATION

Parents may be notified in a number of ways. The school or district may use its broadcast phone or text message system. In some cases, students may be asked to send a text message to their parents. A reunification text message from a student may look something like this: *"The school has closed, please pick me up at 3:25 at the main entrance. Bring your ID. "*

PARENT/GUARDIAN EXPECTATIONS

If a parent or guardian is notified that a controlled release and reunification is needed, there are some expectations that parents or guardians should be aware of. First, bring identification. That will streamline things during reunification. Second, be patient. Reunification is a process that protects both the safety of the student and provides for an accountable change of custody from the school to a recognized custodial parent or guardian.

WHAT IF A PARENT CAN'T PICK-UP THEIR STUDENT?

When a parent can't immediately go to the reunification site, students will only be released to individuals previously identified as a student's emergency contact. Otherwise, the school will hold students until parents can pick up their student.

WHAT IF THE STUDENT DROVE TO SCHOOL?

There may be instances where a student may not be allowed to remove a vehicle from the parking lot. In this case, parents are advised to recover the student. In some circumstances, high school students may be released on their own.

Reunification Information (PLEASE PRINT CLEARLY)
Have photo identification out and ready to show school district personnel.

Student Name ....

Student Grade .... Student Cell Phone Number ....

Name of person picking up student ....

Signature ....

Phone number of person picking up student .... | School personnel completes: Photo identification matches name of person picking up student? Yes or No

Relationship to student being picked up ....

Parent/Guardian completes:
Print Student Name Again .... Student Grade ....

Teacher .... School personnel completes upon release of student

Student Birthday .... | TIME | INITIALS | OTHER

HOW IT WORKS

For students, the school asks that students be orderly and quiet while waiting. Students may be asked to text a message to their parents or guardians. Students are also asked not to send other text messages either in or out of the school or reunification area. Keeping the cellular network usage at a minimum may be important during a reunification.

REUNIFICATION CARDS

For parents, there are a couple of steps. If a parent is driving to the school, greater awareness of traffic and emergency vehicles is advised. Parents should park where indicated and not abandon vehicles. Parents are asked to go to the Reunification "Check In" area and form lines based on the first letter of their student's last name. While in line, parents are asked to fill out a reunification card. This card is perforated and will be separated during the process. Some of the same information is repeated on both the top and separated bottom of the card. Parents are asked to complete all parts of the card.

In the case of multiple students being reunified, a separate card for each student needs to be completed.

BRING ID TO CHECK IN

During check in, identification and custody rights are confirmed. The card is separated and the bottom half given back to the parent.

From the "Check In" area parents are directed to the "Reunification" area. There, a runner will take the bottom half of the card and take it to the Student Assembly Area to recover the student or students.

Parents should be aware that in some cases, they may be invited into the building for further information.

INTERVIEWS AND COUNSELING

In some cases, parents may be advised that a law enforcement investigation is underway and may be advised that interviews are necessary. In extreme cases, parents may be pulled aside for emergency or medical information.

SRM Signage

FAQs

FREQUENTLY ASKED QUESTIONS

Since introducing the Standard Reunification Method in 2012, thousands of districts, departments, and agencies have scrutinized, evaluated, and ultimately implemented the program. During the process, some questions seem to come up often.

SERIOUSLY, WHAT DOES IT REALLY COST?

Since its introduction in 2009, public K12 schools, districts, departments, and agencies were free to use The "I Love U Guys" Foundation programs at no cost.

In 2015, the Foundation expanded availability and now offers the programs to any public or private organization at no charge. Simply download the materials and begin the process.

DO WE NEED TO BUY TRAINING IN ORDER TO USE THE PROGRAMS?

No. We've attempted to put enough material online so that schools and law enforcement can successfully implement Foundation programs. We know of thousands of schools across the US and Canada that have implemented the programs using internal resources.

That said, part of our sustainability model relies not just on charitable giving, but on providing training for districts, departments and agencies. If your organization is interested in Foundation training, please contact us for rates and terms.

CAN I MODIFY MATERIALS?

Some details may need to be customized to your location. For instance, the classroom poster should be modified to include hazards and safety strategies that are specific to your location.

ARE THE SOURCE MATERIALS AVAILABLE?

Yes. Some of the materials are available. Original, digital artwork can be provided to organizations that have signed a "Notice of Intent" or a "Memorandum of Understanding" with The "I Love U Guys" Foundation.

Please note: Currently, we are migrating most documents to Pages on the Mac.

CAN YOU SEND ME MATERIALS IN MICROSOFT WORD?

With the exception of the Reunification Operation Kit, no. Retaining the graphic integrity of the materials proved beyond our capabilities using Microsoft Word.

CAN I REALLY USE THE MATERIALS? WHAT ABOUT COPYRIGHTS AND TRADEMARKS?

Schools, districts, departments, agencies, and organizations are free to use the materials under the "Terms of Use" outlined in this document.

DO I NEED TO ASK PERMISSION TO USE THE MATERIALS?

No. You really don't need to ask permission. But, it would be fabulous if you let us know that you're using our programs.

DO I HAVE TO SIGN AN MOU WITH THE FOUNDATION?

It is not necessary to sign an MOU with the Foundation, but please consider it. The Foundation is committed to providing programs at no cost, yet program development, enhancement and support are cost centers for us. One way we fund those costs is through private grants and funding.

An MOU is a strong demonstration of program validity and assists us with these types of funding requests.

DO I HAVE TO SEND A NOTICE OF INTENT?

In the absence of an MOU, a Notice of Intent provides similar value to us regarding demonstrations of program validity to potential funders.

DO I HAVE TO NOTIFY YOU AT ALL THAT I AM USING THE SRM?

We often speak with school safety stakeholders who have implemented the SRM but hadn't mentioned it to us. Please, please, please let us know if your school, district, department, or agency is using the SRP.

It is our goal that the SRP becomes the "Gold Standard." The more schools, districts, departments, and agencies that we can show are using the program, the greater the chance of achieving our goal.

CAN I PUT OUR LOGO ON YOUR MATERIALS?

Yes. But with some caveats. If you are a school, district, department, or agency you may include your logo on posters and handouts. If you are a commercial enterprise, please contact us in advance with your intended usage.

In some states, we have curriculum adoption agreements with "umbrella" organizations. In those states, we ask that you also include their branding.

WE WOULD LIKE TO PUT THE MATERIALS ON OUR WEBSITE.

Communication with your community is important. While you are free to place any material on your website, it's preferable that you link to the materials from our website. The reason for this is to allow us to track material usage. We can then use these numbers when we seek funding.

But, don't let that be a show-stopper. If your IT group prefers, just copy the materials to your site.

Made in the USA
Middletown, DE
26 September 2023

39300689R00022